MW01602357

Weather BINGO

Includes:
- 3x3 Grid
- 25 BINGO Cards
- 18 Calling Cards
- One Sheet of Markers

ANN K. BISHOP

Classroom Star

© Classroom Star All rights reserved.
Permission to copy for personal and single classroom use only.

Directions:

CUT: Adults should cut out call sheets, BINGO cards, and marker sheet from book. Marker sheet can be copied to accommodate as many children as needed. Cut the call sheet into separate images. Cut marker sheet(s) into separate images. (*TIP:* BINGO cards can be laminated for future use.)

HAND OUT: Provide BINGO card and marker images to each child.

PLAY: Determine and describe winning pattern to children. Caller should pull out one image from selection container. Describe the image and show it to the children.

MARK: Children should place marker image on the called image.

HAVE FUN!

POSSIBLE WINNING PATTERNS:

Black Out BINGO - all images must be marked.

Lines BINGO - must make a horizontal, diagonal, or vertical line to get a BINGO.

Squares BINGO - must make the shape of a square along outside edge of card.

T BINGO - must make a capital letter T either right-side up, upside down, or sideways.

U BINGO - must make a letter U either right-side up, upside down, or sideways.

© Classroom Star All rights reserved.
Permission to copy for personal and single classroom use only.

Calling Cards

Sunshine

Earth

Clouds

Rain

Lightning

Sprinkles

© Classroom Star

Weather BINGO 3x3
© Classroom Star

Calling Cards

Rainbow

Snow

Ice

Wind

Fog

Cold

© Classroom Star

Calling Cards

Hot

Wind Sock

Umbrella

Rain Boots

Forecast

Meteorologists

© Classroom Star

Weather BINGO 3x3

© Classroom Star

Markers

© Classroom Star

Weather BINGO 3x3

© Classroom Star

WEATHER BINGO

Rain

Lightning

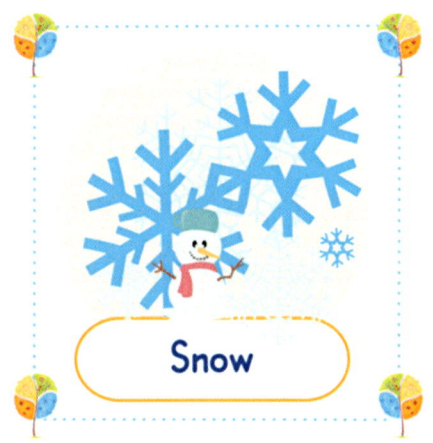

Snow

Cold

FREE

Earth

Ice

Umbrella

Sprinkles

© Classroom Star

Weather BINGO 3x3

© Classroom Star

WEATHER BINGO

 **Snow**	 **Fog**	 **Rainbow**
 **Hot**	**FREE**	 **Rain Boots**
 **Cold**	 **Forecast**	 **Ice**

© Classroom Star

Weather BINGO 3x3
© Classroom Star

WEATHER BINGO

 **Meteorologists**	 **Hot**	 **Lightning**
 **Sprinkles**	**FREE**	 **Clouds**
 **Rainbow**	 **Earth**	 **Ice**

© Classroom Star

Weather BINGO 3x3
© Classroom Star

WEATHER BINGO

Clouds	 Fog	 Sprinkles
 Cold	FREE	 Rain Boots
 Wind Sock	 Sunshine	 Rainbow

© Classroom Star

Weather BINGO 3x3
© Classroom Star

WEATHER BINGO

 Rainbow	 Cold	 Umbrella
 Rain Boots	FREE	 Snow
 Fog	 Earth	 Lightning

© Classroom Star

WEATHER BINGO

Ice

Rain Boots

Wind Sock

Sunshine

FREE

Rainbow

Meteorologists

Clouds

Earth

© Classroom Star

© Classroom Star

WEATHER BINGO

 Rainbow	 Earth	 Lightning
 Fog	FREE	 Wind
 Rain	 Hot	Clouds

© Classroom Star

Weather BINGO 3x3
© Classroom Star

WEATHER BINGO

 **Umbrella**	 **Sunshine**	 **Wind Sock**
 **Fog**	**FREE**	 **Forecast**
 **Sprinkles**	 **Cold**	 **Ice**

© Classroom Star

Weather BINGO 3x3

© Classroom Star

WEATHER BINGO

Rainbow

Rain

Umbrella

Hot

FREE

Earth

Cold

Rain Boots

Meteorologists

© Classroom Star

Weather BINGO 3x3
© Classroom Star

WEATHER BINGO

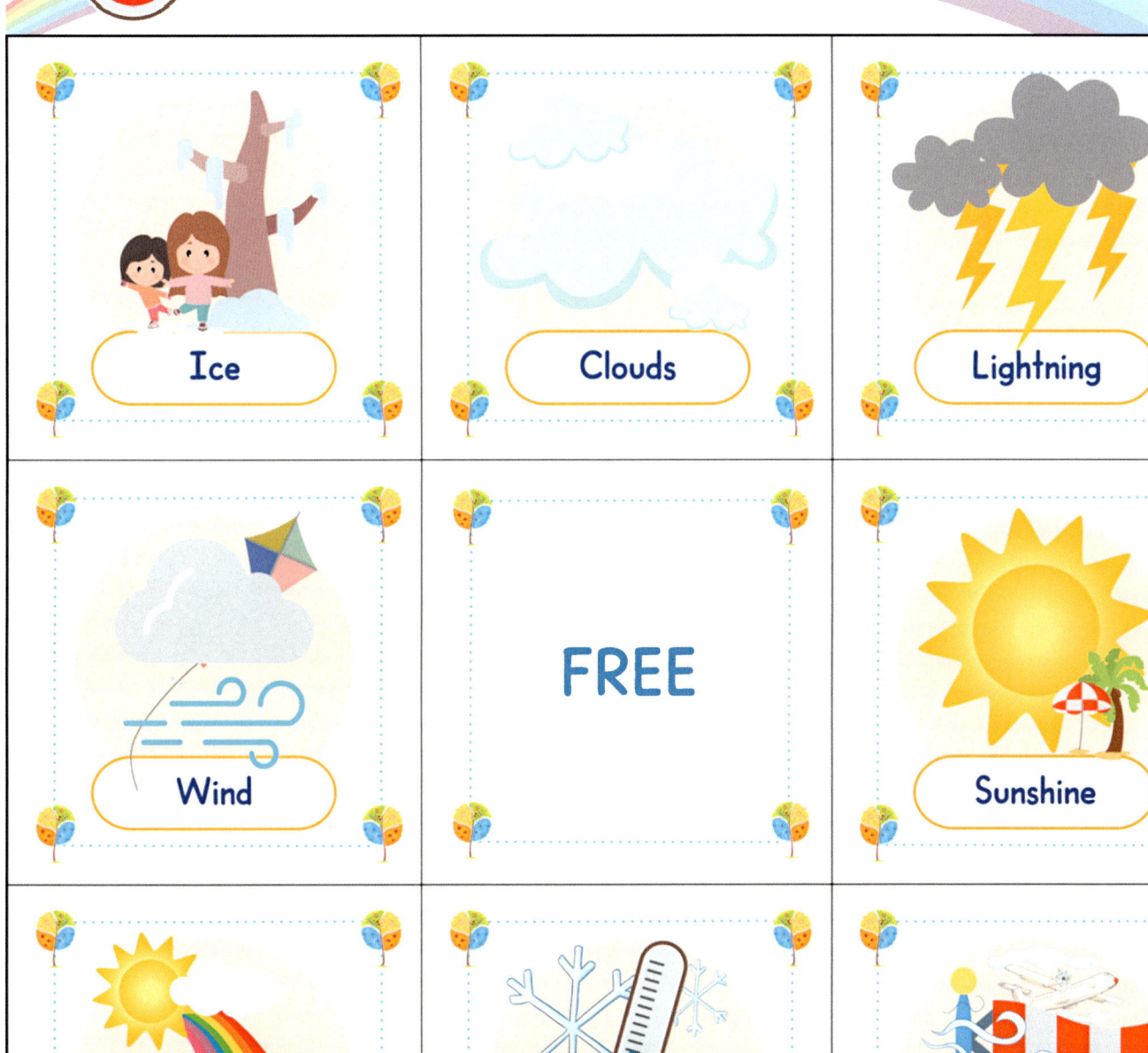

Ice	Clouds	Lightning
Wind	FREE	Sunshine
Rainbow	Cold	Wind Sock

© Classroom Star

WEATHER BINGO

 Ice	 Wind Sock	 Hot
 Cold	FREE	 Meteorologists
 Rainbow	 Earth	 Umbrella

© Classroom Star

Weather BINGO 3x3
© Classroom Star

WEATHER BINGO

 Ice	 Fog	 Lightning
 Wind Sock	FREE	 Forecast
 Rain Boots	 Clouds	 Meteorologists

© Classroom Star

Weather BINGO 3x3
© Classroom Star

WEATHER BINGO

 Cold	 Rain	 Sunshine
 Forecast	FREE	 Wind
 Rainbow	 Snow	 Lightning

© Classroom Star

Weather BINGO 3x3
© Classroom Star

WEATHER BINGO

 **Sunshine**	 **Sprinkles**	 **Rain Boots**
 **Wind Sock**	**FREE**	 **Meteorologists**
 **Umbrella**	 **Wind**	 **Lightning**

© Classroom Star

Weather BINGO 3x3
© Classroom Star

WEATHER BINGO

Meteorologists	Lightning	Ice
Hot	FREE	Clouds
Rain	Wind	Fog

© Classroom Star

Weather BINGO 3x3
© Classroom Star

WEATHER BINGO

 **Hot**	 **Rain Boots**	 **Earth**
 **Rainbow**	FREE	 **Snow**
 **Sprinkles**	 **Ice**	 **Wind**

© Classroom Star

WEATHER BINGO

Rain Boots	Rain	Lightning
Earth	FREE	Forecast
Umbrella	Wind Sock	Ice

© Classroom Star

Weather BINGO 3x3

© Classroom Star

WEATHER BINGO

 Meteorologists	 Rain	 Rainbow
 Rain Boots	FREE	 Hot
 Cold	 Clouds	 Lightning

© Classroom Star

WEATHER BINGO

Fog	Earth	Ice
Cold	FREE	Sunshine
Meteorologists	Sprinkles	Rain

© Classroom Star

Weather BINGO 3x3

© Classroom Star

WEATHER BINGO

Earth

Forecast

Ice

Clouds

FREE

Cold

Rainbow

Lightning

Sunshine

© Classroom Star

Weather BINGO 3x3
© Classroom Star

WEATHER BINGO

Fog	Rainbow	Earth
Hot	FREE	Rain Boots
Ice	Meteorologists	Wind

© Classroom Star

Weather BINGO 3x3
© Classroom Star

WEATHER BINGO

Sprinkles	Forecast	Rain Boots
Fog	FREE	Earth
Ice	Rain	Rainbow

© Classroom Star

Weather BINGO 3x3
© Classroom Star

WEATHER BINGO

Clouds	 Ice	 Earth
 Sprinkles	FREE	 Sunshine
 Rain	 Wind	 Meteorologists

© Classroom Star

© Classroom Star

WEATHER BINGO

 **Rain**	 **Umbrella**	 **Wind Sock**
 **Forecast**	**FREE**	 **Sunshine**
 **Snow**	 **Clouds**	 **Rain Boots**

© Classroom Star

WEATHER BINGO

Clouds

Umbrella

Wind

Rain

FREE

Meteorologists

Ice

Earth

Fog

© Classroom Star

Weather BINGO 3x3

© Classroom Star

Did you enjoy this BINGO book?

If so, I'd love to hear about it.

Please share your review so others can find this book, too.

Every kind review really helps!

Thank you.   Ann K.

Made in United States
Orlando, FL
04 March 2025

59163008R00038